THIS BOOK BELONGS TO:

_____

The CHOSEN
for kids

40 DAYS WITH
JESUS
BOOK ONE

BroadStreet
KIDS

BroadStreet Kids
Savage, Minnesota, USA

BroadStreet Kids is an imprint of BroadStreet Publishing® Group, LLC.
Broadstreetpublishing.com

The CHOSEN for Kids

© 2023 by The Chosen, LLC.

9781424564798
9781424564804 (eBook)

Devotional entries composed by Amanda Jenkins and Tara McClary Reeves.
Art direction and design by Kristen Hendricks and Amanda Jenkins.
Editorial services provided by Michelle Winger.

Printed in China.

23   24   25   26   27   5   4   3   2   1

A Note for Parents

This book is for younger kids. And older kids. And all the years in between. Which means there will be words that are hard. And words that are easy.

Encourage your children to ask you questions if there are things they don't understand. Better still, read with them! Go through this devotional at the dinner table or before bed. Talk through the questions and pray as a family.

Whether kids read on their own or with you, our hope and prayer is for them to grow in the knowledge and love of Jesus.

Can we get an "Amen"?

Introduction

You are about to read a book written by two students (who just-so-happen to be 40 and 50 years old), because you're never too old or too young to study God's Word!

As moms, we care about two things: That by reading this book, 1) you'll know how much Jesus loves you, and 2) you'll grow more every day in your desire to love Him back.

As a companion to *The Chosen's 40 Days with Jesus* devotional series for grownups, this book will help you—along with your parents—discover the joy, peace, and wonder found only in a forever friendship with Him.

Day 1

Before

Before God ordered time to march in minutes, you were on His mind. Yes, you. You're not here by luck, by accident, or as the result of a giant explosion. You're here because of God's divine choosing. Your Creator carefully selected you. And you were made to live in His love.

That said, you're not perfect and you don't always make good choices. None of us do. Like the ancient Israelites who came before us, our hearts want to wander, and we don't always obey the God who loves us. We may nod our heads in agreement with the Bible, but then we sometimes do the opposite of what it says. But guess what? God never gives up on us. He never gives up on *you*.

Sure, you're going to mess up, but making miracles out of messes is God's specialty. Just ask Mary Magdalene who, for a little while, was ruled by demons. But Jesus rescued her and made her part of His core group of followers.

Or ask Simon Peter. He believed his only success in life came from catching loads of fish. But Jesus made him a "fisher of men" instead, meaning Simon Peter brought many people to his Savior.

Or ask Nicodemus whose whole identity came from his fancy religious robes and perfect church attendance. But Jesus taught him what it means to truly follow God from the inside out.

And don't forget math-whiz Matthew who was obsessed with making money. But Jesus helped him see that a relationship with his Savior was the only treasure worth counting.

Like Mary Magdalene, Simon Peter, Nicodemus, and Matthew, God wants you to love Him. His love isn't dependent on what you do, how you wear your hair, how many friends you have, if you're good at sports, or if you get straight As. He has loved you from the very beginning—even before the beginning of time.

And that's a love you can trust.

Prayer Time

Praise God for loving you since before the world was made. Ask Him to help you trust His love and to believe you're special simply because He says you are. Thank Him for calling you to follow Jesus, just like He did with Mary Magdalene, Simon Peter, Nicodemus, and Matthew.

What's Next?

God loved you long before this moment and He's going to love you for all the moments to come. How does knowing that make you feel? How might it change the way you respond to Him today?

Based on Book 1, Day 1

Day 2

Words

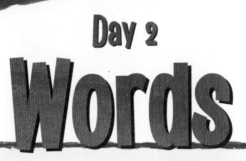

Before the world began, there was the Word. The Word was
with God, and the Word was God. He was with God in the
beginning. All things were made through him.
Nothing was made without him.

John 1:1-3

Jesus is not a created being whose existence began in His
mother's womb. He's eternal and He has always lived alongside God the
Father in heaven. John called Him, *The Word* who was "with God in the
beginning" to help us understand Jesus' role in creation. In the beginning
God spoke and everything in the world came to be, including things like
bananas and butterflies, rabbits and rain, flowers and freckles
(Genesis 1-2).

Better still, because the Creator's character is perfect, He cannot think, say, or do anything wrong. He's always good. So, although you sometimes may not understand God's ways, you can trust His words. He promises, "Never will I leave you" (Hebrews 13:5 niv), which means there's no better friend than the One who made you.

Jesus loves you. And just like His disciples, He wants you to experience Him on a deeper level. Consider Andrew and his brother, Simon Peter. They grew up hearing the special promises of God about a coming Savior. So, when Jesus arrived and said the words, "Follow me, and I will make you fishers of men," they did! They left their nets and their boat to go with the One who spoke the world into being (Mark 1:16–18).

It's hard to imagine dropping everything for something so new and unknown. But it makes sense because Jesus *is* life, and His words are like light that chases away the darkness. His words drive out fear and confusion. His words bring comfort and understanding. In fact, Jesus' words help us know what's important.

Including how important you are to Him.

Andrew and Simon Peter took Jesus at His Word and responded to His call. And then the brothers made it their mission to bring others to Jesus too. They weren't the same after meeting Him. Nobody is. When Jesus says the words, "Follow Me," and you obey, He moves you from darkness to light, from death to life, from an empty net to a full heart because He is indeed the living Word.

Prayer Time

Ask God to give you the courage of Andrew and Simon Peter to (1) say yes to Jesus' words, "Follow Me," and to (2) introduce one of your friends to Him today. Before you even try, thank Him for giving you the right words to say and for preparing the heart of whoever He has placed on yours.

What's Next?

What might you say to bring someone closer to Jesus?

Based on Book 1, Day 4

Hope

> But the angel said to him, "Zechariah, don't be afraid. Your prayer has been heard by God. Your wife, Elizabeth, will give birth to a son. You will name him John."
>
> Luke 1:13

You may be having a good day today but, no matter who you are, there are tough times ahead. Parents are going to let you down. Friends might gossip behind your back. You may break a bone or fail a test or have an illness that doesn't go away.

Whatever the day brings, the Bible (which is called "God's Word" because it's full of His words!) gives us HOPE no matter the circumstances.

Consider this. Between the Old and New Testaments, the Israelites experienced 400 years of silence from God—which was really hard because they were used to God's words being regularly delivered by the Lord's chosen messengers.

Can you imagine how many times they must have read and re-read the Old Testament during those years? And everything from Genesis to Malachi pointed to a Savior, so God's people were extremely anxious for Him to come.

During those days, there was a couple whose names were Zechariah and Elizabeth. They loved God and continued to trust Him even through the silence because their hope wasn't in the things they experienced; their hope was in the Lord. After all, they had studied His Word from long ago.

One day, Zechariah was visited by a messenger from God: the angel Gabriel. Zechariah was afraid...because of course he was! How would *you* feel if an angel showed up in *your* room? But Gabriel told Zechariah he had nothing to fear. He had happy news from the Lord: "You and your bride, Elizabeth, are going to have a baby!"

And with that, the silence of God was broken.

Unfortunately, Zechariah believed some of God's message but not all. He doubted and said, "We're too old to have a baby!" But Gabriel reminded him that God's words are always true, so for nine months Zechariah was unable to speak.

Now *he* was the silent one.

As Elizabeth's belly grew, so did her husband's understanding that nothing is impossible with God (Luke 1:37). In fact, God had chosen this very old couple to raise John the Baptizer, the man who was going to prepare the people for the Savior they'd been waiting for.

Jesus, the hope of the world.

Prayer Time

Thank God for the hope you have because He is able to do anything and everything. So, even if things are hard right now, ask the Lord to help you trust Him. Ask the Lord to be your hope.

What's Next?

It's okay to have doubts, but God wants you to bring your questions to Him. He loves you no matter what. What are some areas in your life where, like Zechariah, you're doubting God's promises? How does Luke 1:37 encourage you?

Based on Book 1, Day 8

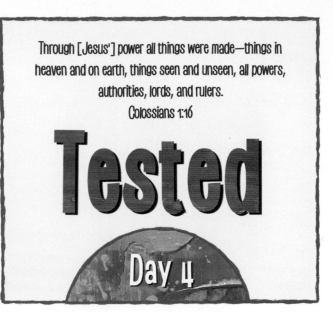

Through [Jesus'] power all things were made—things in heaven and on earth, things seen and unseen, all powers, authorities, lords, and rulers.

Colossians 1:16

Tested

Day 4

Imagine you're taking a test. Your teacher wants to see how well you remember the information you recently studied. You're stuck on one of the questions and your neighbor's paper is so close... You know cheating is wrong, so, although you really want to peek at your schoolmate's answers, you resist.

Well done, kid.

To be clear, being tempted isn't a sin. But giving into temptation is.

Have you ever stopped to think about the difference between a test and a temptation? God may test you, but He will never tempt you. Testing reveals how much we know about God and how willing we are to trust in

His strength to get us through hard things. Temptation, on the other hand, is meant to lead us *away* from God.

And getting people to move away from God is the devil's business.

Picture the scene. John the Baptizer was standing right next to Jesus in the Jordan River. God had just announced that He loves His Son and was well-pleased with Him (Mark 1:9-11). So, you might think an after-party was planned with lots of food and friends to celebrate the moment. Nope. Instead, Jesus was led by the Holy Spirit into the desert where there was no cake. Or ice cream. Or celebrating.

In the wilderness that day, Jesus came face-to-face with His enemy, the fallen angel who rebelled against God because he thought he was better (Isaiah 14:13-14). And so, Satan was punished and cast out of heaven and hurled to earth (Ezekiel 28:15-17)—which sounds scary because we live here, but the truth is that the devil is on a leash. There's only so much he can do and, in this particular showdown, Jesus reminded Satan of his limitations.

Spoiler alert: There is no limit to Jesus' power. He ranks higher than everything that has been made, including Satan (Colossians 1:15).

After 40 days without food, Jesus' stomach was growling. Since Satan strikes hardest when people feel weakest, he tempted Jesus to stop fasting and praying and to satisfy His own appetite. But Jesus didn't bite. He used the Word of God to defeat every temptation from the enemy and demonstrated that when you depend on God's promises, provision, and power, you're a star student.

No matter if you're twelve years old or a hundred and twelve, tests and temptations are part of life. The devil is always going to tempt you, but God's Word will lead you in the way that is right. With each second of His life, Jesus proved that trusting His heavenly Father is always the best answer.

Prayer Time

Thank God for sending Jesus to show you how to respond when Satan tempts you to do wrong. Ask the Holy Spirit to give you the strength to make wise choices.

What's Next?

Look up Matthew 4:1-11 in your Bible. What Old Testament book did Jesus quote to answer Satan's questions? Name a few verses you can memorize to help you when you're tempted.

Based on Book 1, Day 10

Jesus went to Capernaum, a city in Galilee. On the Sabbath day, Jesus taught the people. They were amazed at his teaching, because he spoke with authority.

Luke 4:31-32

Day 5

Authority

One day, Jesus introduced Himself like this: "Truly, truly, I say to you, before Abraham was, I AM" (John 8:58 esv).

Say what? Did this guy just claim to be God?!?

You see, this audience knew there was only one "I AM," and that God had already claimed that special title for Himself (Exodus 3:13-14). The name actually means that God has no beginning or end. He's everywhere and understands everything. He doesn't depend on anyone outside of Himself. It's like He was saying, "I AM every amazing thing your mind can imagine."

So, you can imagine God finishing the sentence with any amazing word: I AM love. I AM light. I AM truth. I AM forgiveness. I AM all-powerful. I AM all-knowing. I AM the King. I AM. I AM. I AM.

When Jesus referred to *Himself* as "I AM," the people freaked out. But even though they didn't like what He said, they had a hard time denying that His words matched what they were seeing. This guy who had grown up in the sleepy town of Nazareth as a simple carpenter was now making sick people well. And the crowds were equally amazed by how Jesus taught with wisdom and authority—because of course He did! The same One who spoke the world into existence was speaking to them.

And they didn't like it one bit.

Why not? Because Bible times were a lot like the world is today. People were arguing over things like politics and religion, and everybody thought they were right. The Jewish leaders were trying to hold onto their power in a system controlled by Rome. And the Romans were trying to control everyone else. Everybody wanted their own authority.

But Jesus didn't come to win an argument or an election or a popularity contest. He came to 1) save people from sin and 2) teach the world how to have a personal relationship with the Great I AM. And the Bible says that one day soon *Jesus will come again* to gather and reward His followers—those who have believed Him and submitted to His authority (Revelation 22:12-13).

Prayer Time

To submit to Jesus means to surrender to His authority in your life. Praise Him for being the Great I AM, your Savior and rightful King. Ask Him to help you trust Him as Lord over everything, including your own heart.

What's Next?

God has placed authority figures like parents in your life to help you, which means you can count on Satan to whisper, "What do *they* know? You're old enough to make your own decisions." Remember, the devil always wants to lead you away from God and His authority. But recognizing Jesus as the Great I AM means you listen and obey Him. So when the Bible says things like, "Honor your father and your mother," you do it (Exodus 20:12)!

Based on Book 1, Day 13

Day 6

Boldness

"So I tell you, continue to ask, and God will give to you.
Continue to search, and you will find.
Continue to knock, and the door will open for you."
Luke 11:9

Every single day, Jesus' followers saw the importance their Master placed on praying and searching for the will of His Father. They wanted to follow His example because they had teachable hearts—which means they didn't act like know-it-alls. They were willing to become wiser by obeying what Jesus said and did.

Including the way He talked to God.

To help His disciples understand prayer, Jesus told a story about a man who was surprised by a friend's late-night visit. Not only did his friend arrive at midnight, he was also really hungry. But there was no food in the pantry. So, the kind man put on his coat and ran to a neighbor's house. By that time it was even later, and the neighbor wasn't very nice. "Go away!" he yelled. But the kind man's friend had a real need, so he didn't stop knocking. Finally, the grouch gave in and shared some supper (Luke 11:5–8).

By telling this story, Jesus was saying, "Guys, if this man's persistent knocking won over his *unloving* neighbor, don't you believe your *loving* Heavenly Father will also answer you?"

You see, Jesus knew many of His followers were discouraged. Maybe they were scared because they didn't have enough money or food of their own. Maybe they had family members back home who were sick. Maybe they wanted to tell people about Jesus but didn't have the right words. Maybe someone they loved had already rejected Jesus and that made them feel sad or afraid.

You may be worrying about a lot of things too, but God wants you to boldly ask Him for whatever you need. Just like Jesus did—and just as He taught His disciples to do—you can ask! In fact, knocking on God's door through prayer demonstrates that you trust Him to be the solution to your problems. Best of all, your confidence in His love and in His willingness and ability to provide makes His heart happy.

Prayer Time

Thank God for always opening the door when you knock and for responding to you in kindness and love. Ask Him to make you more bold in prayer and to notice when He does!

What's Next?

What need are you trusting God to take care of today?

Based on Book 1, Day 14

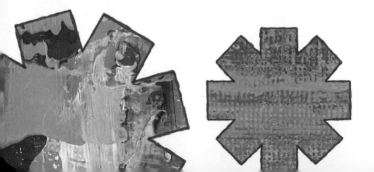

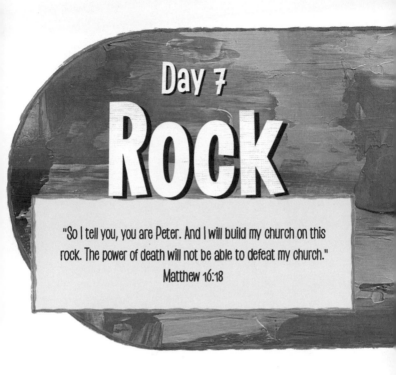

Day 7
ROCK

"So I tell you, you are Peter. And I will build my church on this rock. The power of death will not be able to defeat my church."

Matthew 16:18

When Andrew first introduced Simon to Jesus, Simon was intrigued. He could tell right away this teacher was different, and perhaps even wondered if Jesus was joking when He said, "You are Simon the son of John. [But now] you shall be called [Peter]" (John 1:42 ESV).

The name Peter means "rock".

Well, Simon's arms probably *were* muscular. Pulling up fishing nets day-in and day-out was an effective workout—maybe he flexed. But while Simon Peter might've associated his new title with his outward

appearance, the Bible tells us that God sees inside.

"God does not see the same way people see. People look at the outside of a person, but the Lord looks at the heart" (1 Samuel 16:7).

Jesus knew that Simon Peter was *not* always strong on the inside. On the contrary, he was an emotional, moody guy who often said and did things without thinking.

For example, one day Jesus asked His twelve disciples: "Who do you say I am?" (Matthew 16:15) Without skipping a beat, Simon Peter answered correctly, "You are the Christ, the Son of the living God" (Matthew 16:16). But later when Jesus was arrested (and because Peter was afraid he would be too), he pretended like he didn't even know Jesus (Matthew 26:74).

So, here's the question: If Simon wasn't always strong on the inside, why did Jesus name him "Rock"?

Here's the answer: Because Jesus makes us what we're not.

Jesus knew the choices Simon Peter was going to make even before he made them. But He also knew His beloved disciple would repent, that he had a teachable heart, and that he'd eventually become more like his Savior, the strong and steady Rock of Salvation (2 Samuel 22:47).

And the same can be true for you.

Following Jesus doesn't mean your name is going to change. But over time *your insides will* because the more you spend time talking to Jesus in prayer, reading your Bible, and obeying what it says, the more you'll become like the true Rock of our salvation.

Prayer Time

Give thanks to God for making you more like Jesus. Ask His forgiveness for the times your choices didn't match your calling to follow Him, and invite Him to keep changing you from the inside out.

What's Next?

Read and underline Philippians 1:6 in your Bible. What should you remember next time you mess up?

Based on Book 1, Day 15

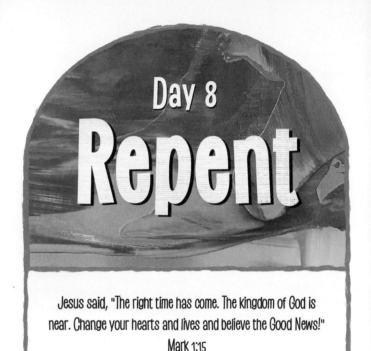

Day 8
Repent

Jesus said, "The right time has come. The kingdom of God is near. Change your hearts and lives and believe the Good News!"
Mark 1:15

One of Satan's favorite schemes is to convince you that you're good enough. He'll get you to count how many Sundays you attend church, how many Bible verses you memorize, or how many kind words you speak to your neighbor. He'll try to make you believe you're good *apart from Jesus* because that way you won't think you need to turn away from sin.

But that's the opposite of what the Bible says. God's Word is clear that the human heart is deceitful (Jeremiah 17:9), that all people have sinned (Romans 3:23), and that we desperately need a Savior (Romans 6:23).

As cute as you were as a teeny tiny baby, and even though you didn't know it yet, your desire was to go away from God, which means your good works can't get you a spot in heaven. Salvation is a gift paid in full by Jesus. You can't earn it with your good choices; it's already free! All you're required to do is accept God's gift.

That's why the word *gospel* means "good news" and why every Christian has a before-and-after story. When you follow Jesus, He changes you to be more like Him and less like the "before" you once were.

Part of Simon Peter's before-and-after story included a fishing trip where he worked all night but caught nothing. Imagine his surprise when a carpenter from Nazareth began telling him—a professional fisherman—how to fish!

"[Jesus] said to Simon, 'Take the boat into deep water. If you will put your nets in the water, you will catch some fish.' Simon answered, 'Master, we worked hard all night trying to catch fish, and we caught nothing. But you say to put the nets in the water; so I will'" (Luke 5:4-5).

By that simple act of obedience to Jesus, the men got to experience a miracle. As soon as their nets hit the water, the catch was bigger than any they'd ever seen. Their boats almost sank! And then so did Simon Peter's knees, right into the sand as he said, "Go away from me, Lord. I am a sinful man" (Luke 5:8).

In that moment, Simon saw his need to turn away from sin because no amount of good choices could cover it up. He knew he was in the presence of God and that his life needed to change. And so, the fisherman willingly laid down his net, repented of his sin, and started following Jesus.

Prayer Time

Confess any sin you need to turn away from. Thank God for His forgiveness and that He's 1) the God of miracles and 2) the author of your before-and-after story.

What's Next?

Share your before-and-after story with a friend or family member.

Based on Book 1, Day 16

Philip found Nathanael and told him...
"We have found [the Messiah]. He is Jesus, the son of
Joseph. He is from Nazareth." But Nathanael said to Philip,
"Nazareth! Can anything good come from Nazareth?"
Philip answered, "Come and see."
John 1:45–46

Day 9
Come and See

The Bible is clear. God's ways are not like ours (Isaiah 55:8–9). His strategy to get His message of salvation to the world included Himself and twelve men who were so different from one another, it made most people scratch their heads! Many of the rough-around-the-edges disciples (who were handpicked by Jesus) were scratching their heads too.

About each other and also about Him.

John and Andrew were the first disciples called, followed by Simon Peter. Philip was next and then he urged Nathanael to also "come and see." But Nathanael was concerned about where Jesus was from—because surely the Savior of the world wasn't going to come from a place like Nazareth.

Truth is, Jesus' hometown wouldn't have made anyone's list of favorite vacation spots. Nazareth was a small town with very few schools or churches. It did have a military base for Roman troops, but they were the last group of people anyone wanted to be around. And all of that made it hard to believe the Savior they'd been waiting for was actually from Nazareth!

Jesus surprised Nathanael by saying, "Here is truly a person of Israel. There is nothing false in him" (John 1:47).

In other words, Jesus knew exactly what Nathanael was thinking. (And that His new recruit didn't usually keep his opinions to himself.)

Nathanael asked, "How do you know me?" Jesus answered, "I saw you when you were under the fig tree. That was before Philip told you about me" (John 1:48).

In other words, Jesus also knew exactly where Nathanael had been.

And suddenly, Nathanael knew that Jesus knows everything! "Teacher, You are the Son of God. You are the King of Israel!" (John 1:49) Because of his willingness to come and see, Nathanael's mind was radically changed, and he became a follower and friend of Jesus.

Do you know that Jesus sees you and knows what you're thinking too, even before you speak? More amazing still is that God loves you anyway and—just as He did with Nathanael—wants to reveal His knowledge and power to *you*. All you have to do is come to Him each day and see what He has in store.

Prayer Time

Thank God for the Bible which allows you to see and know who He really is. Praise Him because He knows everything about you and still wants you to come. Ask Him to help you follow Jesus each day so that your friendship with Him will continue to grow.

What's Next?

Who can you invite to come and see the Lord? Invite a friend, your neighbor, or even a parent to attend church or youth group with you this week.

Based on Book 1, Day 17

Day 10

Worry

"So, don't worry about tomorrow. Each day has enough
trouble of its own."
Matthew 6:34

The first four men Jesus called to follow Him were professional fishermen, and Matthew 4:20 tells us how they responded: "At once [they] left their nets and followed him."

Isn't it interesting that the men left their nets behind?

Truth is, if a fisherman wasn't careful, he could get all tangled up in his net. And the same thing can be true of worry because it has a tendency to tangle us up and choke out the fun—which is not the life God wants for us since following Jesus can actually be fun!

In fact, Jesus' very first miracle occurred at a wedding party. In first century Israel, weddings weren't just one-day events; they lasted an entire week. Jesus and His disciples had been invited to one such celebration along with His mother, Mary. But on day three, the hosts ran into trouble.

Back then, wine was part of most large gatherings. But during this particular party, the wine ran out. Having no wine to serve would've been really embarrassing for the family who was hosting, so Mary was worried about her friends, but she didn't get all tangled up in it! She took the problem straight to Jesus.

"They have no wine," were Mary's words, but her meaning was clear... *Help!*

And Jesus did.

The disciples got to watch as God's Son instructed the servants to fill giant jars with water, which probably seemed strange, but, like the disciples, the servants obeyed at once and the water turned into wine! The party and the people in charge of it were saved (John 2:1–11).

Here's the point: Whenever you take your worry to Jesus, you're setting yourself up for the best possible solution. In fact, your problems are just opportunities for God to work in your life. He understands what you're facing, and He promises to take care of you in all things, big or small. It's your job to take everything to Him and to do what He says.

That way, you'll never miss out on the fun of following Him!

Prayer Time

Ask God to give you the strength and courage to trust Him with your worries. Talk to Him about them—He knows already, but He wants you to pour out your heart to Him.

What's Next?

Talk about a time you watched Jesus transform your worry into joy. You could even start a prayer journal to write down and remember all the ways God takes care of you. Your memory may fail, but you'll see that His faithfulness never does.

Based on Book 1, Day 19

Day 11

Trust

Trust the Lord with all your heart. Don't depend on your own understanding. Remember the Lord in everything you do. And he will [make your paths straight].
Proverbs 3:5-6

What do you want to be when you grow up? An astronaut? A fireman or doctor? A professional singer, NBA star, stay-at-home parent, or an actor on a TV show? Or maybe you have dreams of becoming a tax collector like Matthew.

The last one's a joke.

Being a tax collector in first century Israel was the *last* job. Matthew's parents wanted for their Jewish boy. Why? Well, back then

Rome required payments called taxes for goods and services. The guys who worked for them were not only considered traitors of their Jewish brothers and sisters, they often kept some of the money for themselves as well.

So, no doubt, Matthew was an outcast in his hometown *and* in his family.

But then along came the Lord.

After this, Jesus went out and saw a tax collector named [Matthew] sitting in the tax office. Jesus said to him, "Follow Me!" [Matthew] got up, left everything, and followed Jesus (Luke 5:27-28).

Matthew came to understand there would be no real joy or success in his life apart from Jesus, the real treasure. After all, money hadn't made him happy; indeed, everything he accomplished on his own only hurt the people he loved. So, in that moment, Matthew made the greatest decision of his life by putting his trust in Jesus.

Perhaps it's too early for you to know what you want to be when you grow up, and that's okay. You have a lot of time to pray, dream, and plan before you become an adult. But your main job in life should always be to trust Jesus—and you don't have to wait to start! Belonging to

Jesus doesn't come with an age requirement. God's Word promises that when you choose to believe and obey Him, He will direct your steps.

Just as He did for Matthew.

Prayer Time

Tell God you're sorry for the times you've tried to figure things out on your own instead of following Him. Thank Him for always wanting what's best for you. Ask Him (1) to help you trust Him with your whole heart and (2) to direct all your steps.

What's Next?

Ask a family member or friend to tell you about a time when they trusted the Lord for direction. In what specific ways are you trusting Him today?

Based on Book 1, Day 20

If anyone makes himself clean from evil things, he will be used for special purposes. He will be made holy, and the Master can use him. He will be ready to do any good work.

2 Timothy 2:21

Useful

Day 12

Up until the day Matthew met Jesus, his life was defined by what he did. He probably thought his math skills, ability to read and write, and the work he did for Rome (along with all the money he got doing it) made him valuable. But Matthew's thinking was the opposite of God's thinking.

Jesus didn't choose Matthew because of his talent, money, or anything else in the tax man's life. In fact, here's the word problem Jesus helped the numbers guy solve: "Whoever tries to hold on to his life will

give up true life. Whoever gives up his life for me will hold on to true life" (Matthew 10:39).

In other words, when Matthew confessed his sinfulness and gave his life to Jesus, God gave him a new life and a whole new identity. He was made clean from the inside out the moment he became a child of God. At which point he started doing good works for the kingdom of God!

Same was true for Simon Peter and Andrew. "[The brothers] were fishing in the lake with a net. Jesus said, 'Come follow me. I will make you fishermen for men.' At once Simon and Andrew left their nets and followed him" (Matthew 4:18-20).

Same was true for Mary Magdalene. "There were also some women with [Jesus] who had been healed of sicknesses and evil spirits. One of the women was Mary, called Magdalene, from whom seven demons had gone out... The women used their own money to help Jesus and his apostles" (Luke 8:2-3).

Same is true for you.

Maybe you're confused about your purpose in life. Maybe you've believed the lie that your value comes from what you're good at rather than who God is making you to be. But don't be fooled. The Master is indeed making you holy, which means to be cleaned from the inside out and set apart for Him.

Want even more good news? Like Matthew, Simon Peter, Andrew, and Mary, God wants to use you to tell others about Jesus and what He can do for them too.

Prayer Time

Praise God for cleansing you from sin and for making you new. Thank Him for giving His followers good works to do, and ask Him to help you find your true value and purpose in Him.

What's Next?

Read more stories about heroes of the faith like Deborah (Judges 4–5), David (1 Samuel 17), and Paul (Acts 9, 20:22–24)—just to name a few—who God made new and used in mighty ways.

Based on Book 1, Day 21

Many people believed in [Jesus] because they saw the miracles he did. But Jesus did not believe in them because he knew them all. He did not need anyone to tell him about people. Jesus knew what was in a person's mind.
John 2:23-25

Day 13
Relationship

Jesus sees and understands everything. He knows the feelings you feel and the thoughts you think—and He loves you anyway. In fact, Jesus came to have a relationship with you. He wants to be your friend, and friends spend time together.

Just stop for a moment and think about that. The King of all kings wants to hang out with you. That should blow your mind!

Sadly, Jesus dealt with a lot of people who only wanted to hang out with Him because of the miracles He performed. They'd swallow a

fish sandwich and then follow Him around for another (John 6). Okay, maybe not an actual sandwich but you get the idea because people came to Jesus for stuff they wanted.

But Jesus doesn't want you to love Him for what He can do for you—which is anything. He wants you to love Him for who He is—which is everything.

In the Gospel of Luke, Jesus met ten men who were suffering with a skin disease called leprosy that forced them to live far away from their homes and families. They begged Jesus to heal them and He did, but only one returned to say thank you; which means only one guy in the whole group understood that a relationship with God isn't about the presents... it's about spending time in His presence (Luke 17:11–19).

Truth is, every single day Jesus does amazing things for you. He gives you food to eat and air to breathe. He causes the sun to rise and set, and He keeps watch over you all the minutes in between. Most importantly, He heals the disease in your heart called sin so that you can be part of His family.

Some people might say they love you to the moon and back. But Jesus loves you to the tomb and back. He died for you and then rose again, proving that a relationship with Him will never end. That's the best kind of friend you could ever hope to have and *definitely* one worthy of your time.

Prayer Time

Praise God for wanting to spend time with you. Welcome Jesus into the details of your day and ask Him to make you more like the leper: thankful for all God has done and eager to be in His presence.

What's Next?

Make a list of some things you're thankful for right now. If your relationship with Jesus isn't at the very top, come up with some ways to change that. Perhaps you could spend more time reading your Bible, or more time talking to God in prayer, or more time singing songs of praise to Him in the shower. You get the idea.

Based on Book 1, Day 23

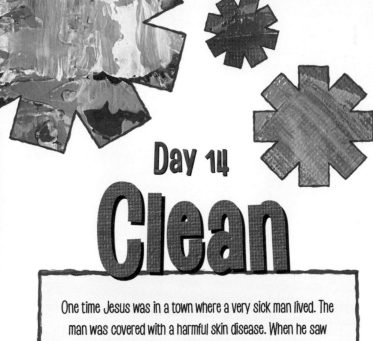

Day 14

Clean

One time Jesus was in a town where a very sick man lived. The man was covered with a harmful skin disease. When he saw Jesus, he bowed before Jesus and begged him, "Lord, heal me. I know you can if you want to."
Luke 5:12

People used to think they could catch leprosy by simply standing next to someone who had it. So, everyone infected with the terrible illness was banned from the community. If a sick person did come close to others, he or she was required by law to shout a warning: "I'm not clean! I'm not clean!" In other words, "I'm comin' through, so you'd better run and hide!"

Can you imagine having to do that? Can you imagine what it would feel like to have everyone in your life run away because they believed you were hopelessly *unclean*? No doubt the lepers in those days felt sad, alone, and afraid.

Except for the one who ran to Jesus.

Instead of shouting the usual warning and staying far away, a man (who heard about all the miracles Jesus was doing) drew near to the Savior. Bowing before his only hope, he begged Jesus to heal him.

Of course, Jesus didn't flinch. "[He] said, 'I want to. Be healed!' And Jesus touched the man. Immediately the disease disappeared" (Luke 5:13).

Although amazing, the best part of this story isn't the healing. The best part is that Jesus reached out and touched the unclean man. He didn't have to; after all, Jesus has the power to just *think* things and they happen. But He knew the man had been alone for a really long time and probably needed a hug—which is exactly why Jesus touched him.

Our Savior is so, so kind.

"But Christ died for us while we were still sinners. In this way God shows his great love for us" (Romans 5:8).

Like the leper, you have a terrible problem called sin that makes your heart unclean. But also like the leper, Jesus is your hope. All that's required for your sin-sick heart to be made clean is to run to Him, bow down, and ask Him to clean you up. Rest assured that when you do, Jesus will say, "I *want* to. Be healed!"

Prayer Time

Draw near to God and praise Him for loving you while you were still a sinner. Ask for His forgiveness and thank Him for making your heart clean. Remember, even after choosing to follow Jesus, we all still sin—which means asking for forgiveness should be a daily thing. But that's okay because so is God's willingness to make us clean!

What's Next?

What part of this story made your heart the happiest? With your words and actions, how can you help the people around you experience more of Jesus' hope, love, and kindness today?

Based on Book 1, Day 24

Day 15
Rise

Some people came, bringing a paralyzed man to Jesus. Four of them were carrying [him]. But they could not get to Jesus because of the crowd. So they went to the roof above Jesus and made a hole... Then they lowered the mat with the paralyzed man on it. Jesus saw that these men had great faith. So he said to the paralyzed man, "Young man, your sins are forgiven."

Mark 2:3-5

The place where Jesus was preaching was packed. Standing room only. No doubt, the paralyzed man would've been happy to stand and listen to Jesus along with everyone else if only he could have. But instead, his four loyal friends had to carry their buddy all the way there. Unfortunately, once they arrived, no one in the crowd was willing to make a path for them to get close to the Healer.

Fast forward a little.

As Jesus spoke, chunks of mud and straw began falling on the heads of His listeners. And when the shocked audience looked up, they saw the four friends lowering their pal through a hole they'd cut in the roof.

Can you imagine being so determined to get to Jesus that you'd scale a wall and come through a ceiling? Jesus was so impressed by their faith that He said to the paralyzed man, "Your sins are forgiven" (verse 5).

To be honest, those were not the words anyone expected to hear and definitely not what the men came for. They came to hear Jesus say, "Your <u>body</u> is healed!"

But Jesus wanted the people to know who He really was and why He really came, so He said, "Which is easier, to say to the paralytic 'Your sins are forgiven'? Or to say, 'Rise, take up your bed and walk'? But that you may know the Son of Man has authority on earth to forgive sins—he said to the paralytic—'I say to you, rise pick up your bed, and go home'" (Mark 2:9-11 esv).

In other words, Jesus came to cure what's sick, broken, and paralyzed on the inside. He healed the man's legs to prove He can heal our hearts and our relationship with God. Which means that just like the men who were willing to trust in and get close to Jesus, you too can receive the greatest healing of all.

And you don't have to scale a wall to get it.

Prayer Time

Praise God for forgiving your sins and ask Him to help you 1) trust Jesus more and 2) be a faithful friend to others by bringing them to Jesus.

What's Next?

Who in your life might be hurting or in need? How can you be a faithful friend to them today?

Based on Book 1, Day 25

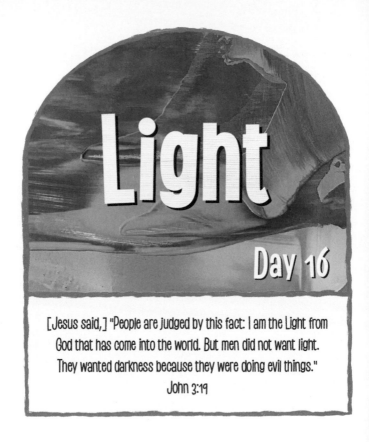

Light

[Jesus said,] "People are judged by this fact: I am the Light from God that has come into the world. But men did not want light. They wanted darkness because they were doing evil things."

John 3:19

A secret meeting under cover of darkness seemed like a good idea to Nicodemus because that way the Pharisees wouldn't wonder whose side he was really on—especially since many of them were plotting how to get rid of Jesus. They didn't like the man from Nazareth who healed the sick and spoke with authority because they thought it threatened their own. And so, it came as no surprise that Nico chose to meet the "Light of the world" in the shadows (John 8:12).

Up until that night, Nicodemus believed obeying rules made him "good." But Jesus explained that anyone who doesn't repent and follow Him is actually stuck in spiritual darkness. Jesus is the light that exposes what lives inside our hearts.

Unfortunately, not everybody wants their sin exposed. But Jesus wasn't just a healer, and He definitely wasn't just a nice guy who taught good things; He was the Savior of the world who Nicodemus and all the other religious folks had been studying for centuries. And contrary to their popular opinion, the Messiah hadn't come to set the Jewish people free from Rome; He came to set us all free from sin and darkness.

Including rule-followers like Nicodemus.

Maybe you're like a lot of churchgoers who think obeying rules is enough to make you good, and that your choices somehow cover the sin that hides inside your heart. Or maybe you're like the Pharisees who resisted Jesus because, like them, you don't want to obey Him at all. Or maybe you're like Nicodemus and you worry what your friends will think if they catch you following God's one and only Son.

But God doesn't want you to be stuck in the dark. That's why Jesus came! He wants you to move into His light, repent of your sin, and then stay there safe in His gracious, cleansing, loving presence.

Thank goodness that after Jesus' death on the cross, Nicodemus no longer hid. In front of everyone, He helped prepare Jesus' body for burial. And three days later, he got to hear the glorious news that Jesus had risen from the dead, proving that death, sin, and darkness were forever defeated by Christ's eternal love and light.

Prayer Time

Thank God for sending Jesus as a light to rescue you from the darkness of sin.

What's Next?

Take a moment to describe light. How is Jesus like light in your life?

Based on Book 1, Day 30

> "For God loved the world so much that he gave his only Son. God gave his Son so that whoever believes in him may not be lost, but have eternal life."
>
> John 3:16

Day 17

Believe

John 3:16 is one of the most well-known Bible verses in the world. It was spoken by Jesus to Nicodemus during their secret meeting at night—which clearly means their meeting didn't stay a secret!

Truth is, Nicodemus was an impressive guy. He was powerful and popular, successful and smart. He had knowledge of God's promises, from Genesis to Malachi. But the Old Covenant that was described in the Old Testament was written to point Nicodemus and the whole wide world to Jesus.

Jesus is the New Covenant written about in the New Testament.

New and new... but more on that in a minute.

No doubt Nicodemus was familiar with Isaiah 53:6: "We all have wandered away like sheep. Each of us has gone his own way. But the Lord has put on him the punishment for all the evil we have done." Perhaps as a boy, Nico even stood in front of his parents or grandparents and recited that verse from memory.

But knowing is not the same as believing.

Before he met Jesus, Nicodemus thought his ability to recite Scripture and perform his religious duties were good works that would help get him into heaven. But he was wrong because, as we've been discussing, the Bible says being good doesn't earn God's forgiveness or favor. Only believing in Jesus and what He did on the cross can remove the punishment for all the evil we've done.

And so, it's not about being good. Or smart. Or successful, powerful, or popular. It's about taking what you've heard and know about Jesus and believing that He's the New Covenant: God's only Son sent to take the punishment for sin, so we can be saved and spend eternity with Him in heaven.

The moment you confess your sins and say YES to Jesus, you're no longer lost; you have eternal life! In Him you're a brand-new person—a new creation with a new mind, a new heart, and a new purpose. And that's exactly what Nicodemus and every other human in the history of humans have longed for.

Whether they believe it or not.

Prayer Time

Praise God for His incredible love that led to Jesus taking the punishment for your sins. If you haven't already, ask Him to help you accept the free gift of salvation. If you have accepted it, ask God to help you grow more and more in faith (*faith* is another word for *belief*!).

What's Next?

What are some of the ways God is making you <u>new</u> as a result of your belief in Jesus?

Based on Book 1, Day 32

Precious

Some people brought their small children to Jesus so he could [bless] them. But his followers told the people to stop bringing their children to him. When Jesus saw this, he was displeased.

Mark 10:13–14

Mothers, fathers, and grandparents were bringing boys and girls to Jesus to be blessed and healed by Him. But the disciples were blocking the young ones from coming.

Who would do that?!

We aren't actually told why the men were turning children away. Perhaps they thought Jesus was too important or busy to be bothered by a bunch of kids. But Jesus said, "Let the children come to me. Don't stop them! The Kingdom of God belongs to those who are like these little children" (verse 14).

Jesus made it clear that children have a very special place in His heart. In fact, you're so precious to God that He wants older people to be more like *you*—to be humble, kind, and eager to spend time with Him.

Truth is, it's easier for kids to slow down and spend time with Jesus than it is for their parents... easier to enjoy God's creation, to rest in His love, and to listen to His words. No doubt the children who were brought to Jesus that day wanted to be with the one who made them feel precious.

Precious things have great value and are treated with care, which is exactly how Jesus treated children and how He wants to treat you too. He wants to spend time with you. He knows how important and wonderful you are because He made you!

Maybe you don't feel precious to Jesus. People often don't. Maybe you don't think you're smart enough or pretty enough to be valuable. Maybe you don't think you have enough friends, money, talent, or trophies to be special to anyone, let alone the King of the universe.

But if you think those things, you're wrong. You are precious to Jesus. And each and every day He wants you to come to Him and experience His forgiveness, His total acceptance, and His unconditional love.

You are welcome. You are wanted. And God has exciting things to share with you about the wonderful adventure He has planned *just for you*, His precious creation.

Prayer Time

Praise God for making you and for declaring you precious. Thank Him for wanting to spend time with you. Accept that invitation today and all the days.

What's Next?

Write out Luke 12:6-7 and display it somewhere you'll regularly see it because it's important to remind yourself again and again how special you are to Jesus.

Based on Book 1, Day 34

Created

In Christ Jesus, God made us new people so that we would do good works. God had planned in advance those good works for us. He had planned for us to live our lives doing them.

Ephesians 2:10

Alexander Graham Bell invented the telephone so people could be in two different places but still communicate. The Wright Brothers made the airplane to get travelers from one city to another faster than they could by car or train. Ruth Wakefield came up with the chocolate chip cookie to give to people who stayed at her inn.

Each new creation made an impact on history. But the designers used raw materials—things that had already been made—to get their inventions to work. God, on the other hand, is so awesome that He

creates things out of nothing. He simply speaks the word, and what He imagines comes into existence! And everything God makes has tremendous purpose behind it.

Including the way He made you.

And including the way He made the Old Testament prophet, Jeremiah.

God said to Jeremiah, "Before I formed you in the womb I knew you, before you were born, I set you apart. I appointed you as a prophet to the nations." But Jeremiah felt insecure about his assignment. He said, "I do not know how to speak; I am too young." So, the Lord said, "Do not say, 'I am too young.' You must go to everyone I send you to and say whatever I command you. Do not be afraid of them, for I am with you and will rescue you" (Jeremiah 1:4–8 niv).

God's message to Jeremiah is the same one He has for you: You are God's special design, uniquely created 1) to know Him and 2) to point others to Jesus.

Want even more good news? God promises to give His Holy Spirit to you the moment you choose to follow Jesus, to live inside your heart and help you do the good work He created in advance for you to do!

And so, you don't have to feel insecure or afraid. Ever.
God made you. He'll be with you. And He will help you.

Prayer Time

Thank God for creating you. Ask Him to help you believe you were uniquely made to do the good works He planned even before you were born.

What's Next?

What good work do you feel the Holy Spirit prompting you to do? To encourage someone who's sad or forgive someone who's wronged you? To spend more time with God? To tell someone that they too have been uniquely made?

Based on Book 1, Day 37

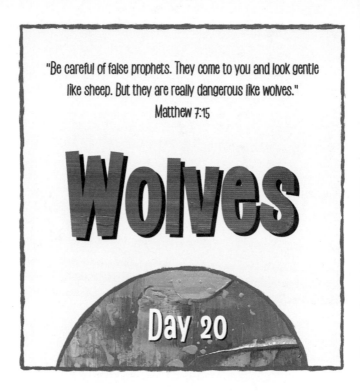

"Be careful of false prophets. They come to you and look gentle like sheep. But they are really dangerous like wolves."
Matthew 7:15

Wolves

Day 20

Wolves are predators. That means they survive by eating other animals. They're sneaky and they make surprise attacks. Lambs, on the other hand, are defenseless and easy to catch, which makes them a favorite snack for wolves. And so, the job of a shepherd is extremely important. Shepherds protect the sheep, and there's nothing they won't do to keep their flock safe.

Jesus compared false teachers to wolves, and He warned His

followers about being tricked by them. You see, instead of telling people what they NEED to hear, false teachers tell people what they WANT to hear, filling their ears and minds with lies. For example, a false teacher might say that Jesus is one of many ways to get to heaven. But Jesus said He's the only way to get to heaven (John 14:6).

Can you see how dangerous a lie like that could be?

Jesus also compared Himself to shepherds. In fact, He called Himself "The Good Shepherd," and *you*, dear reader, are one of His precious sheep (Psalm 100:3). There's nothing He won't do to protect you; He proved that on the cross when He took the punishment for sin so you could spend eternity with Him in heaven. He loves you that much, and He wants you to enjoy the incredible life He has planned for you in the kind of peace and safety only He provides.

So how can the flock of Jesus spot a sneaky, lying wolf?

By staying close to the Good Shepherd, of course! The more you talk to God in prayer, the more your ears will be trained to hear what's true and what's not. The more time you spend reading the Bible, the more your mind will know the difference between what's right and wrong. And when the things you're hearing or seeing are wrong, run from them just like you'd run from a hungry wolf, right back to the Shepherd who loves you.

"I am the good shepherd. The good shepherd lays down his life for the sheep." John 10:11 niv

Prayer Time

Thank the Lord for being your good shepherd. Ask Him to give you the ability to recognize what's true and what's false. Ask Him to protect you from wrong teaching and thinking, so that you can live in the peace and safety of His truth. And then praise Him for loving you enough to lay down His life for you, His precious sheep.

What's Next?

According to 2 Timothy 4:3-5, what should you continue to do, no matter what "wolves" say?

Based on Book 1, Day 38

"But whoever drinks the water I give will never be thirsty again. The water I give will become a spring of water flowing inside him. It will give him eternal life."
John 4:14

Day 21
Wellspring

It was the hottest part of the day in the desert of Samaria—an area most Jews preferred to walk around instead of through. Not because of the harsh landscape, mind you, but because of the rocky relationship between Jews and Samaritans. And yet, the Bible says Jesus *had to* go through Samaria (John 4:4).

Interesting choice of words, don't you think?

Tired from the long journey, Jesus sat by Jacob's well just as a Samaritan woman arrived to draw water—and the timing was no coincidence. You see, divine appointments (otherwise known as encounters with God) often take place when we least expect them.

No doubt, the Samaritan woman assumed this day would be like every other. She'd take her empty bucket—along with her empty heart—to the well where she had sent it down and pulled it back up a hundred times before. Then she'd carry the heavy load of water all the way home.

But this day *wasn't* like any other. When she arrived, Jesus was there. And He asked her for a drink. Of course, she was surprised by His question because in Bible times it wasn't normal for a man to talk to a woman in public. It definitely wasn't normal for a Jew to ask a Samaritan for help. And it for sure wasn't normal for Jesus to reveal some of her secrets—the sin she wanted to hide.

But Jesus wasn't trying to embarrass her. Rather, He wanted her 1) to see her need for a Savior and 2) to know that He was the Savior! Because just like our physical bodies need water to survive, God created our hearts to thirst for Him—if only we'd go to Him to be filled.

Jesus called Himself *living water* because He's the only true source of forgiveness, healing, peace, joy, hope, and salvation. He's like a wellspring that never runs dry. He's like a water bucket that always stays full. He's not like anyone or anything else. And in this moment that was divinely appointed by the God who loved her, the Samaritan woman was about to figure that out.

The woman said to him, "I know that [the Savior] is coming." Jesus said to her, "I who speak to you am he." John 4:25-26 esv

Prayer Time

Praise God for sending Jesus to be your wellspring of salvation. Thank Him for being willing to fill your heart and satisfy your soul. Ask that He'd help you choose to spend time with Him every day in order to be refreshed and renewed.

What's Next?

What are some things you thought would "fill you up" and make you happy, but ultimately didn't? A new outfit or video game? More friends or better grades? Why do you think the excitement wore off so quickly? Who is the only one the Bible says can deeply satisfy your heart?

Based on Book 1, Day 39

Day 22

Lonely Place

But Jesus often slipped away to other places to be alone so that he could pray.

Luke 5:16

Being around other people is fun, but it's still important to spend quiet time alone with God. He wants you to talk to Him in prayer, to read your Bible, and to obey what it says.

These are habits that please the Lord.

A habit is something you do regularly like making your bed, brushing your teeth, or walking your dog. But there are probably times you skip healthy habits and choose the bad ones instead. Things like binging on sugar, picking your nose, or spending too much time in front of the TV. Thing is, most of the choices you make are either helpful or harmful to you in the long run.

Because choices have consequences.

Jesus is our perfect example of how to make godly choices. Every day He demonstrated the importance of talking to and hearing from His heavenly Father. He said, "For I have come down from heaven, not to do my own will, but the will of him who sent me" (John 6:38 esv).

The time Jesus spent with God directed His choices.

It may seem hard to find a quiet place and even harder to listen for God's voice. After all, we don't hear Him speak in the same way we hear others. But that's why it's so important to make time with Him a habit. The more you read your Bible and pray, the more your spiritual ears begin to hear.

Just like David's.

We don't know exactly what the king was facing when he wrote Psalm 25, but it's obvious he was having a hard time. David asked God: "Turn to me and be kind to me. I am lonely and hurting. My troubles have grown larger. Free me from my problems" (16–17).

Clearly, David spent time with God, sharing his thoughts and asking for help. In fact, the Bible describes him as "a man after God's own heart," because he pursued God's heart (1 Samuel 13:14). Like Jesus, he made a habit of spending time with the Lord and listening for His voice.

And God wants you to do the same because it's usually in the quiet places—in the solitary, even lonely places—where followers of Jesus begin to understand He's the *only* one who can really help. The one who fills our emptiness, changes our circumstances, and teaches us how to respond.

That's why spending time with Him should be your #1 habit!

Prayer Time

Praise Jesus for being your example of how to step away from others to be with God. Ask Him to help you establish godly habits, starting with your time. Thank Him for listening and responding to you and for never leaving you alone.

What's Next?

Find a special time and place to be on your own. Look up a few verses like Joshua 1:9, Isaiah 41:10, and John 14:18. Pray them back to God and thank Him for always being there for you.

Based on Book 2, Day 3

Day 23
Riddles

[Jesus] said, "Listen! A farmer went out to plant his seed....
Some seed fell on rocky ground where there wasn't much dirt.
The seed grew very fast there because the ground was not
deep. But when the sun rose, the plants withered. The plants
died because they did not have deep roots. Some other seed
fell among thorny weeds. The weeds grew and choked the good
plants. So those plants did not make grain. Some other seed fell
on good ground. In the good ground, the seed began to grow."

Mark 4:2-8

Jesus often spoke to large crowds in parables, which are earthly
stories that teach heavenly lessons. The people who trusted in Him
worked hard to understand the meaning of the parables. When they
were confused by something Jesus said or did, they kept following Him
and asking more questions. They sought to understand. And so, in time,
they did.

On the other hand, the people who did *not* trust in Jesus didn't understand and didn't try to. Instead, they dismissed His stories as riddles. Kind of like seeds that fall on rocky soil.

One day, a large group gathered around Jesus near the Sea of Galilee where He was sharing a parable called, "The Sower and the Seed." In those days most people planted and grew their own food, so they knew how important it was to scatter seeds in the best, most fertile soil.

Good soil helps seeds to grow.

Unfortunately, Jesus knew there were people listening to Him whose hearts were like rocky soil that causes seeds to die. Their stubbornness to believe was crowding their hearts, leaving no room for deeper roots of faith to grow.

He also knew there were people listening to Him whose hearts were like soil full of thorny weeds. Weeds have the ability to choke and ultimately kill good plants, just like worries about life or loving money can actually "choke" and destroy a person's faith.

Thankfully, Jesus also knew there were people listening whose hearts were like good soil, where seeds of faith would grow deep, strong roots. People with faith like that don't stop following Jesus when life gets hard—they move closer to him. People with faith like that don't choose stuff over Jesus—they willingly give up all things for more of what He offers.

So what's the point of Jesus' parable?

To check your heart. Jesus wants you to consider the condition of your heart to make sure it is "good soil" ready to soak up His words. That doesn't mean you won't have questions. It means that when you do, you'll ask for help—you'll seek to understand.

And over time, your roots of faith will grow deep and strong.

Prayer Time

Ask God to 1) help you understand His words and 2) give you the courage to keep following even when you're confused. Praise Him that in time (and just like He did with the early disciples), He will help you understand—and grow!

What's Next?

Think about the different types of soil Jesus talked about in Mark 4:1-20. Which one best describes your heart right now?

Based on Book 2, Day 6

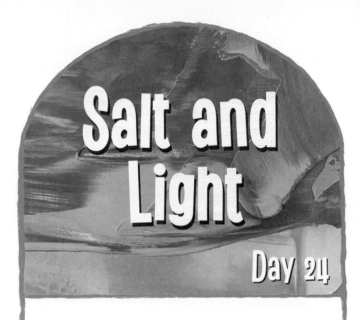

Salt and Light

Day 24

"You are the salt of the earth. But if the salt loses its salty taste, it cannot be made salty again. It is good for nothing. It must be thrown out for people to walk on. You are the light that gives light to the world. ...people don't hide a light under a bowl. They put [it] on a lampstand. Then the light shines for all the people in the house. In the same way, you should be a light for other people. Live so that they will see the good things you do. Live so that they will praise your Father in heaven."

Matthew 5:13–16

Becoming a follower of Jesus is the greatest decision you'll ever make, but it comes with great responsibility too because Jesus wants you to be salt and light.

Say what now?

Salt does a lot of things. It adds flavor to many of your favorite meals. It's a preservative, which means it makes food last longer by stopping the growth of germs. And salt can also make you thirsty.

But what does that have to do with following Jesus? Well, like salt, Christians add flavor to the world by being joyful, peace-filled, and bold in their faith. We also help preserve the world by refusing to give into temptation and by sharing the love of Jesus with others. And when we live like that, people watching become "thirsty" for a relationship with Him too.

Light, on the other hand, does one main thing.

It chases away the darkness.

Of course, that's why we don't hide lights under bowls; that would be silly because it would defeat the whole purpose of light! Rather, we put light on display so we'll know which way to walk. Light invites people to come out of the darkness. It keeps us safe because it makes us see.

Like light, Jesus wants His followers to shine brightly for Him, so others will know which way to walk. He wants you to stand up for what's good and true. He wants you to glow with warmth and kindness and acts of service to others. And He wants the hope you have to draw others to Him too, thereby chasing away the darkness of sin and death.

Jesus wants people to know you're different because of Him. So, be salty for Jesus and shine, kid! Let your relationship with Him flavor your every sentence and shimmer in your every step.

It's what He's calling you to do.

Prayer Time

Praise the Lord for drawing you to Himself. Ask Him to help you to be salt and light to the people around you, and to be different for Him in all the wonderful ways He's helping you to be.

What's Next?

What are some new ways you can be salty and bright for Jesus today?

Based on Book 2, Day 7

"Love your enemies. Pray for those who hurt you. If you do this, then you will be true sons of your Father in heaven. Your Father causes the sun to rise on good people and on bad people. Your Father sends rain to those who do good and to those who do wrong.

If you love only the people who love you, then you will get no reward.... If you are nice only to your friends, then you are no better than other people. Even people without God are nice to their friends. So you must be perfect, just as your Father in heaven is perfect."

Matthew 5:44-48

Love

Day 25

One day Jesus taught His followers a really hard lesson that went something like this: If you want to be like Jesus, love everyone. Even your enemies.

YIKES.

But Jesus wasn't asking His followers to do something He wasn't already doing. In fact, the prophet Isaiah told us way back in the Old Testament that Jesus would be treated badly.

People made fun of Him and even His friends left Him (Isaiah 53:3). And yet, Jesus didn't show anger or try to get even. Instead, He did exactly what He taught His followers to do. He was kind. He was gentle. He prayed for His enemies even when they hung Him on a cross.

"Jesus [was] taken to a place called the Skull. There the soldiers nailed [him] to his cross... Jesus said, 'Father, forgive them. They don't know what they are doing'" (Luke 23:33–34).

If Jesus was kind and gracious to the people who were actually putting Him to death, certainly we can be kind to people who are unkind to us. Yet it still feels so impossible because, truth be told, loving our enemies *is impossible* without God's help!

That's the secret to loving your enemies: you must rely on God's strength to obey. The power and patience to love others who seem unlovable doesn't come from you; it comes from the one who is love (1 John 4:16). The one who saved you and is changing you from the inside out.

In Philippians 4:13 you are promised, "I can do all things through Christ because he gives me strength." If you've accepted Jesus, the Holy Spirit lives inside you to help you do the hard things you can't imagine doing on your own. Things like loving your enemies and praying for those who've hurt you. Simply put, the ability to love comes from God who is perfect and who is in the process of making you more and more like Jesus.

Prayer Time

Praise the Lord for His perfect love and for His promise to help you love those who are unloving toward you.

What's Next?

Who do you currently feel is an enemy and how can you obey God's instruction to love that person anyway?

Based on Book 2, Day 8

Day 26
Prayer

> One time Jesus was praying in a place. When he finished, one of his followers said to him... "Lord, please teach us how to pray, too."
> Luke 11:1

The disciples didn't ask Jesus how to teach; they asked Him how to pray. Clearly, they saw the difference prayer made in the life of their leader, and they wanted what He had.

To pray is to have a conversation with God: to share our hearts and to experience His. It's a way to show God how much we love Him, value His direction, and desire His wisdom. It's also a way to worship: to praise God for who He is and the things He's done.

Prayer is *not* reciting a list of things we want—even though that's often what we do. Instead, prayer is the opportunity to tell our loving heavenly Father how we feel and to listen for Him to tell us how to be.

That said, sometimes we don't know *what* to say. And that's okay. Like the disciples, we can let Jesus be our teacher. He answered them:

Pray like this,
Our Father in heaven, (Acknowledge that God is over all things.)
May Your name be kept holy. (Agree that God is perfect.)
May Your Kingdom come soon, may Your will be done on earth,
as it is in heaven. (Call on God to do what HE wants.)
Give us today the food we need, (Ask for what you need.)
And forgive us our sins, (Repent of any sin in your life.)
As we have forgiven those who sin against us. (Forgive others.)
And don't let us yield to temptation (Ask for help to resist sin.)
But rescue us from the evil one. (See Matthew 6:9–13.)

Prayer shouldn't feel like a script, and the words you say can be your own. But Jesus was giving His followers a guideline for how to interact with their heavenly Father. Of course, as your circumstances change, so will your prayers. Some days you'll feel sad. Other days you'll feel happy. And God wants to hear all of it! But Jesus demonstrated that prayer shouldn't be about us alone, and that God deserves our praise, obedience, and trust.

Prayer Time

Ask the Lord to guide you as you pray. Thank the Holy Spirit for praying for you, which is totally amazing (Romans 8:26–27), and for growing you into a person who makes talking *and listening* to God part of every day.

What's Next?

Write down your prayer today. Remember, you can use your own words, but maybe try using Jesus' guideline: acknowledge, agree, call, repent, ask. Notice how different your prayers become when you do!

Based on Book 2, Day 9

Day 27
Treasure

"Store your treasure in heaven. The treasures in heaven cannot be destroyed by moths or rust. And thieves cannot break in and steal that treasure. Your heart will be where your treasure is." Matthew 6:20–21

What's something you treasure? Something you *really* love? Maybe it's a piggy bank you've filled and emptied a dozen times. Maybe it's a baseball card collection or a trophy you earned. Maybe it's a necklace you got from a friend. Or maybe it's something your grandparents passed down that was precious to them.

As special as those things are, Jesus wants you to know nothing is more valuable than your relationship with Him. And that God is keeping *actual* treasure for you in a room in heaven.

Yep, you heard that correctly. Those who follow Jesus have treasure being collected and stored up in heaven—which means living for Jesus (believing His words and obeying what He says) is the absolute best thing you could do on earth.

In fact, the Bible says that one day you'll receive "the [treasure] God has for his children. These blessings are kept for you in heaven. They cannot be destroyed or be spoiled or lose their beauty" (1 Peter 1:4).

When you put your trust in Jesus and become God's child, you're automatically granted a treasure that's out of this world. Literally! And that's awfully good news because that piggy bank on your bookshelf will likely crack someday. Your baseball cards will warp and discolor over time. You'll probably lose your necklace at some point, and maybe even that thing Grandma gave you.

That's just the way life goes. Like the Bible says, earthly things don't last. They get ruined and spoiled. They lose their beauty.

The more you understand that, the less you'll love what's temporary. The less you love what's temporary, the more you'll love Jesus. And the more you love Jesus, the more your mind will be able to imagine and truly desire the heavenly things He's setting aside just for you.

So, welcome God's plan and purpose for your life. Accept His forgiveness and extend it to others. Show your sister love *even* when she tattles, and be kind to your brother *even* when he steals the remote control. Because when you follow Christ's example, you're depositing riches into your eternal bank account where treasure lasts forever.

Prayer Time

Ask God for opportunities to grow your heavenly riches by loving Jesus more and by loving and serving others. Thank Him for heaven and for all the special things He has in store for you there.

What's Next?

What are some ways you can store up treasure in heaven today?

Based on Book 2, Day 11

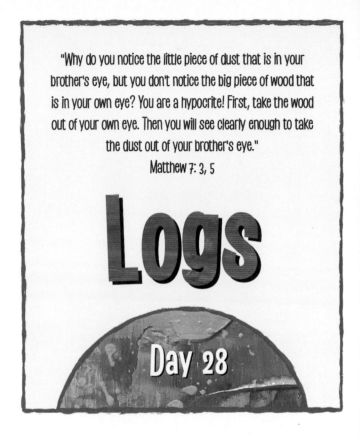

"Why do you notice the little piece of dust that is in your brother's eye, but you don't notice the big piece of wood that is in your own eye? You are a hypocrite! First, take the wood out of your own eye. Then you will see clearly enough to take the dust out of your brother's eye."

Matthew 7: 3, 5

Logs

Day 28

Eye exams are a necessary part of life because being able to see clearly is really *really* important. A doctor can tell whether or not you have good eyesight by showing you a black-and-white letter chart. If you can see all the letters, your vision is good. If you struggle to see some of the letters, you probably need glasses.

Now imagine the doctor who gives you an eye exam has a giant log sticking out of his eyeball. First of all, OUCH. Second of all, wouldn't you wonder why he didn't take care of *his* problem before trying to help you with yours?!?

Jesus used a funny illustration about a little speck of dust and a large log to reveal a vision problem we all have... weak "I" sight. Meaning, each of us has a tendency to pay close attention to the small flaws in other people while ignoring the major flaws in ourselves.

Simply put, we don't see our own logs—our own sin—clearly.

Jesus warned that when we're blind to our sin, we're hypocrites. Hypocrites are people who pretend to make good choices when they sometimes don't. Hypocrites aren't honest with themselves or anyone else. Hypocrites allow sin to remain because they're not willing to repent or make the necessary changes to remove it. And so, hypocrites can't help other people because they're stuck in a mess of their own making.

That's why Jesus instructs, "Take the wood out of your own eye. Then you will see clearly enough to take the dust out of your brother's eye" (Matthew 7:5).

So, how can you remove the log from your own eye and avoid being a hypocrite?

By taking a long, hard look in the mirror. Not an actual mirror because, unlike giant logs, sin isn't something you can see on the

outside. Instead, look into the mirror of God's Word and ask Him for help 1) to not judge others, 2) to see your own sin clearly, and 3) to repent of it and change.

Then and only then will you be able to help those around you.

Prayer Time

Praise God for loving you too much to let you act in ways that are inconsistent with His. Confess the times you've been concerned about other people's flaws instead of your own and pray Psalm 139:23-24: "God, examine me and know my heart. Test me and know my thoughts. See if there is any bad thing in me. Lead me in the way you set long ago."

What's Next?

When you're tempted to criticize the flaws in others, what should you do instead?

Based on Book 2, Day 13

[Jesus] said, "I am the light of the world. The person who follows me will never live in darkness. He will have the light that gives life."
John 8:12

Day 29
Light Source

If you're not plugged into a relationship with Jesus, you might as well be living in the dark. And darkness can be scary because it represents everything that is the *opposite* of God. Things like sadness, anger, rage, confusion, fear, laziness, jealousy, hatred, and even death.

Kinda makes you want to flip on a switch, right?

Just as electricity flows through a lamp when it's plugged in, the moment you invite Jesus into your heart, God's goodness, power, and love flow through you.

Because Jesus is God.

In Genesis 1:3, God said, "Let there be light," and immediately there was light. In Exodus 13:21, God led His people out of slavery and through the wilderness by a pillar of fire. In Exodus 27:20, God commanded the people to always keep lamps burning inside the Tabernacle (God's holy tent) where His presence dwelt.

God is light and gives light. So, when Jesus told the people that He was "the light of the world," He was actually claiming to be God. He was also claiming to give life.

The apostle John described it like this: "[Jesus] was with God in the beginning. All things were made through him. Nothing was made without him. In him there was life. That life was light for the people of the world. The Light shines in the darkness. And the darkness has not overpowered the Light" (John 1:2–5).

Jesus is the source of light and life. Once we know Him, we have no reason to fear the darkness. The Bible says even the darkness isn't dark to God; that darkness and light are the same to Him (Psalm 139:12). He's God. Of course He can't be overpowered by darkness!

And when we follow Him, neither can we.

So, Christian, shine bright! Empowered by the Holy Spirit that lives within you, you can show others the way by telling them about Jesus and inviting them into the light. Because in the same way plants can't live without sunlight, people can't truly live without SONlight.

Plug into His power and watch His light impact the world.

Prayer Time

Thank God for sending Jesus into this dark, sin-sick world. Thank Him for being your light source, and for showing you the way to go. Ask Him to help you shine with His warmth and brilliance so that those around you would see Him too.

What's Next?

What are some ways Jesus' light guides you?

Based on Book 2, Day 15

Test Question

Jesus looked up and saw a large crowd coming toward him. He said to Philip, "Where can we buy bread for all these people to eat?" (Jesus asked Philip this question to test him. Jesus already knew what he planned to do.)

John 6:5–6

Jesus never tests us because He wants to hurt us. Rather, He tests us to display His power in us. He knows He's the answer to life's challenging questions. And in this particular gospel story, the Teacher wanted His students to know it too.

Large numbers of people were following Jesus around to hear Him preach and see Him heal—and as a result, they lost track of the time. The hour was late and the people were hungry. But how on earth were the disciples supposed to feed more than 5,000 men, women, and children?

We're guessing Philip didn't volunteer to answer that question, but he was the one Jesus called on. Of course, Jesus wasn't picking on Philip. He wasn't trying to embarrass or shame him at all. Jesus was giving Philip the opportunity to look to Him for a solution.

Unfortunately, like most of us, Philip's first response wasn't to ask Jesus for help. Instead, the disciple looked to what he had—his own mind, his own money, his own creativity—and it wasn't enough. Not by a long shot.

Philip quickly realized that without Jesus, some things are impossible. But he was about to experience that WITH Jesus, nothing is impossible.

"Jesus said, 'Bring the bread and the fish to me.' Then he told the people to sit down on the grass. He took the five loaves of bread and the two fish. Then he looked to heaven and thanked God for the food. Jesus divided the loaves of bread. He gave them to his followers, and they gave the bread to the people" (Matthew 14:18-19).

Jesus showed Philip and the rest of the doubtful dozen that He is the answer to all of life's questions. He multiplied the loaves and fish enough for every person to eat until they were full. And there were still twelve baskets of leftovers! Which means, Jesus didn't just provide; He provided abundantly.

It also means that He's more than enough to help with whatever you're facing.

Bottom line: the answer is Jesus.

Prayer Time

Praise Jesus for being the solution to life's most challenging problems. Thank Him for being willing to display His power through you. Ask Him to help you be a student who asks honest questions and who looks to God for the answers.

What's Next?

What is a problem you've been trying to solve yourself? What should you do instead?

Based on Book 2, Day 17

Day 31
Follower

> Then Jesus said, "I am the bread that gives life. He who comes to me will never be hungry.
> He who believes in me will never be thirsty."
>
> John 6:35

There are no coincidences with God. So, the fact that Jesus was born in a manger—which was a food trough for barn animals—*means something.* Perhaps God was reminding everyone that just like His creation needs physical food to survive, our spiritual bodies need to be fed and filled by Jesus.

After all, Jesus is "the Bread of Life."

Perhaps when Jesus called Himself that, His audience was reminded of the manna—the bread from heaven—that God provided for the Israelites in the wilderness. Every day, the food they needed to survive simply appeared for them on the ground (Exodus 16).

Or perhaps they remembered how God fed Elijah by having ravens repeatedly bring him meat and bread (1 Kings 17:2-6). Or the widow whose bread-making supplies never ran out (1 Kings 17:12-16). Or how Jesus made a meal for thousands of people with only five loaves and two fish (Matthew 14:13-21).

As amazing as those miracles were, breakfast, lunch, and dinner don't keep your belly satisfied for long. You eat and feel full only to become hungry again because your body burns up the calories you consume.

But when you choose to follow Jesus—to spend time with Him, to listen to Him, to "feed" on His words and "drink" in His presence—your spiritual emptiness is filled and you feel satisfied in the deepest part of your soul.

Are you shaky with insecurity?

Following Jesus provides unconditional love. "[Nothing] in the whole world will ever be able to separate us from the love of God that is in Christ Jesus our Lord" (Romans 8:39).

Are you fidgety over a friendship at school?

Following Jesus provides peace. "My peace I give you. I do not give it to you as the world does. So don't let your hearts be troubled. Don't be afraid" (John 14:27).

Do you have a hankering for happiness?

Following Jesus provides joy. "I have told you these things so that you can have the same joy I have. I want your joy to be the fullest joy" (John 15:11).

Are you faint with fear over where you'll spend eternity? Following Jesus provides certainty. "I give them eternal life, and they will never die. And no person can steal them out of my hand" (John 10:28).

Prayer Time

Praise Jesus for being your soul food. Thank Him for filling your empty heart and ask Him to teach you 1) to follow Him more faithfully and 2) to feast on His Word.

What's Next?

Name one or two ways you can follow Jesus more faithfully today.

Based on Book 2, Day 19

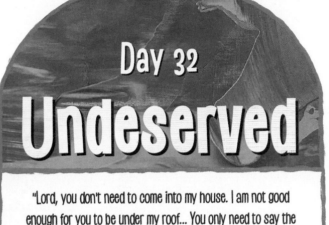

Day 32
Undeserved

"Lord, you don't need to come into my house. I am not good enough for you to be under my roof... You only need to say the word, and my servant will be healed."
Luke 7:6-7

Some words just go together. Like peanut butter and jelly, cream and sugar, bacon and eggs, cookies and milk.

And also grace and mercy.

Grace means you get the royal treatment even when you royally mess up. Mercy means you don't get the punishment your mess-up merits.

Truth is, you're not good enough for God's grace and mercy, which is exactly why those two words are so wonderful! They are gifts from God. You cannot earn them, buy them, barter for them, or bribe God to get them.

No one is worthy. Not even the Roman Centurion that everyone loved.

You see, back in Jesus' day, Jews hated Romans. Rome had captured Israel and then controlled the land by sending soldiers into every city. So, when a group of Jewish elders asked Jesus to help a Roman, it was a very unique situation.

"The men went to Jesus and begged him saying, 'This [Roman] officer is worthy of your help. He loves our people, and he built us a synagogue'" (Luke 7:4-5).

Clearly, the guy did some good stuff. He was kind to the Jews and he built them a place to worship. So, when his servant became sick to the point of death, this Roman asked his Jewish friends *to ask Jesus* for help.

But instead of just asking, the men tried to convince Jesus to heal based on the goodness of their friend. They told Jesus, "He's worthy of your help."

Except he wasn't worthy because no one is. The Bible actually says, "All people have sinned and are not good enough for God's glory" (Romans 3:23).

So, the officer said, "'Lord, I am not good enough for you to be under my roof... [but] you only need to say the word, and my servant will be healed.' When Jesus heard this, he was amazed. He turned to the crowd following him and said, 'I tell you, this is the greatest faith I have seen anywhere, even in Israel'" (Luke 7:6-9).

Jesus isn't impressed with your effort to be "good" because no amount of it can earn you God's favor or a spot in heaven. Only faith in the goodness of Christ can do that.

And the Roman Centurion knew it. He simply asked Jesus to help, and then grace and mercy flowed. His servant was healed, and Jesus demonstrated to everyone watching that faith in Him is all that's required.

Prayer Time

Tell the Lord how grateful you are for His gifts of grace and mercy. Thank Him for the good things He does for you every day and especially for taking the punishment your sin merits.

What's Next?

Make a list of the things in your life that are the result of God's grace and mercy to you.

Based on Book 2, Day 22

Day 33

Amazing Jesus

An effective soldier understands who's in charge, and he's willing to follow orders no matter how difficult or dangerous the mission. He willingly submits to his authority.

Truth be told, submission (which means to yield to another person, to give in, to surrender control) is not a very popular word. Most of us think *we* know what's best, and we don't like being told what to do.

But submission is a requirement for those who follow Jesus.

When the Roman officer found out Jesus was coming to his home, he tried to stop Him. Not only did he believe he was unworthy of the visit, but he also trusted the Savior's authority even from a long way off. He knew all Jesus had to do was say the word and his sick servant would be healed.

Because Jesus is amazing.

The Bible tells us the centurion's comment actually amazed Jesus. Meaning, He loved seeing such a strong, submissive faith. "[Jesus] turned to the crowd following him and said, 'I tell you, this is the greatest faith I have seen anywhere, even in Israel'" (Luke 7:9).

It was quite a compliment. Because as much power as the Roman officer had, he was still humble, trusting, obedient, and confident that Jesus could do what he was asking. In spite of his own great authority, he eagerly surrendered control to the one who was greater.

The question is, are you willing to do the same?

When you choose to follow Jesus, you're saying you surrender to His authority. That you're willing to come when He says come and go when He says go. That you're confident in your Commander in Chief and you trust Him 1) to always do what He says He'll do and 2) to take good care of you.

Prayer Time

Praise God for being worthy of your trust and submission. Thank Him for responding every time you ask Him for help. Ask Him to grant you greater faith and the humility to obey.

What's Next?

Look up Nehemiah 9:6. What does this verse say about our amazing God and why we should submit to His authority?

Based on Book 2, Day 23

Day 34

Ask

We can come to God with no doubts. This means that when we ask God for things (and those things agree with what God wants for us), then God cares about what we say. God listens to us every time we ask him. So we know that he gives us the things that we ask from him.

1 John 5:14-15

Doing awesome things is indeed God's specialty. But sometimes, His answers to your prayers will seem to be the opposite of what you want. Thing is, God wants you to bring your desires, doubts, and worries to Him because He's ready to give you the answers you need.

He, in fact, knows *everything* you need.

All you're supposed to do is ask.

Habakkuk was a prophet in the Old Testament who couldn't figure out why the Lord was allowing bad guys to win, even after he prayed for their wickedness to stop. Habakkuk brought his desires, doubts, and worries—along with his ideas for victory—to God. And when he did, God reassured Habakkuk that the evil around him would eventually be punished.

In God's time and in God's way.

Even though Habakkuk didn't understand God's timing, he knew that God knows everything and that His way is perfect. And that all things, even frightening things, are under His control.

Habakkuk wrote, "But I will still be glad in the Lord. I will rejoice in God my Savior. The Lord God gives me my strength. He makes me like a deer, which does not stumble. He leads me safely on the steep mountains" (Habakkuk 3:18–19).

Habakkuk knew he could ask the Lord for anything and that when those things lined up with what God wanted, God would give Habakkuk what he asked for.

That's the key to asking.

God wants you to tell Him what's on your mind and in your heart. He wants you to ask Him for the things you want. But He also wants you to trust Him to do what's best. And when you ask for what God agrees with, He'll give it to you!

Prayer Time

Praise God because He knows everything. Thank Him for wanting to hear your desires, doubts, ideas, and worries, and for always providing answers in His Word. Ask Him to help you say along with Habakkuk, "I will be glad in the Lord. I will rejoice in God my Savior."

What's Next?

What do you most want to ask God for right now? Knowing He loves you and that He knows everything, are you willing to accept His answer?

Based on Book 2, Day 25

Expectations

John the Baptist was in prison, but he heard about the things the Christ was doing. So John sent some of his followers to Jesus. They asked Jesus, "Are you the man who John said was coming, or should we wait for another one?"
Matthew 11:2-3

John the Baptizer's mission in life was to prepare the hearts of the Jewish people for the coming Savior. In fact, even before he was born, the Bible says John leaped inside his mother's womb when Mary—who was pregnant with Jesus—came near (Luke 1:41).

In spite of the fact that his clothes were made from camel's hair and he ate locusts and he lived in the wilderness, people went to hear his message: "Repent, for the kingdom of heaven is at hand!"
(Matthew 3:2)

Many people *did* repent. Perhaps that's why John thought King Herod would too. But he didn't. Instead, the cruel ruler threw this faithful messenger of the Lord into prison where he stayed for almost two years.

Stuck in that dark jail cell, John began to wonder, *was Jesus really the Savior?*

It was a reasonable question. The baptizer expected the Savior to rescue him from prison. He expected to keep working and preaching and spreading the good news. He expected to live a long life. So, when his expectations went unmet, he began to doubt Jesus.

Be assured that when it comes to your confusion, fear, and doubt, there are no bad questions—as long as you take those questions to Jesus. Which is exactly what John the Baptizer did. "John sent some of his followers to Jesus. 'Are you the [Savior] who is to come, or should we expect someone else?'" (Matthew 11:3 niv)

Jesus wasn't offended by John's question. He didn't criticize him for having doubts or get angry that John was unsure. Instead, Jesus patiently pointed His faithful servant to the proof of His identity.

"Jesus answered, 'Go back to John and tell him about the things you hear and see: The blind can see. The crippled can walk. People with harmful skin diseases are healed. The deaf can hear. The dead are raised to life. And the Good News is told to the poor'" (Matthew 11:4–5).

Jesus not only soothed John's fear, He also turned to the crowd who'd been listening and praised His faithful friend. "I tell you the truth: John the Baptist is greater than any other man who has ever lived" (Matthew 11:11).

Like John the Baptizer, you're going to experience unmet

expectations. There may be days you doubt God's goodness, presence, or love for you. But also like John, you can take your questions to Jesus.

His patience, perfect character, and unconditional love will never let you down.

Prayer Time

Be honest with the Lord about your questions. Ask Him to remind you of who He is and how much He loves you especially when the hard times come. Thank Him for being trustworthy even though you don't always understand His ways.

What's Next?

According to Ephesians 3:17-20, Christ's love for you is "wide and long and high and deep." How does reading about His love change the way you feel when life doesn't go the way you want it to?

Based on Book 2, Day 28

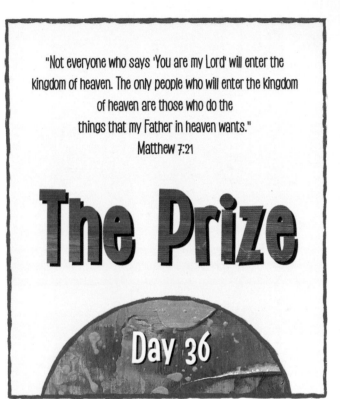

"Not everyone who says 'You are my Lord' will enter the kingdom of heaven. The only people who will enter the kingdom of heaven are those who do the things that my Father in heaven wants."

Matthew 7:21

The Prize

Day 36

Perhaps the saddest words in the Bible are the ones Jesus spoke at the end of His famous Sermon on the Mount: "Get away from me, you who do evil. I never knew you," (Matthew 7:23).

Jesus wasn't declaring that there are people in the world He doesn't love. Or that there are people He doesn't want to save. Romans

10:13 tells us clearly that everyone who calls on the name of the Lord will be saved.

Problem is, some people don't call on the name of the Lord.

Some hear Jesus' invitation to follow but don't accept it because they think they've done too many wrong things. They think they aren't good enough to belong to Jesus. And that's so sad! Because the *only* way for sin to be forgiven is to embrace Jesus as Lord and Savior.

Sadder still is the fact that other people miss the invitation entirely.

Consider Judas. He was one of the twelve men first called to follow Jesus. He probably never skipped a church service. He hung out with Jesus and listened to Him teach for three full years. He saw the miracles and even performed some in the power of Jesus' name. But in his heart, Judas was more focused on making money than on having a real relationship with his Savior.

And he missed the whole point!

The Bible says that unless you turn away from your sinful, self-serving ways to follow Jesus, you will not get the real prize—forgiveness of sin and eternal life with Him.

That's the point. We surrender to Jesus as Lord now in order to spend the rest of our lives with Him in the paradise of heaven! "This is the testimony: God has given us eternal life, and this life is in His Son," (1 John 5:11 niv).

Prayer Time

If you haven't already, pray this prayer:

Dear God,
I'm a sinner. Your Word teaches we all sin. I ask you to forgive me of my sin. I believe Jesus Christ is your Son. I believe you sent Him to earth to die for my sin and that you raised Him to life three days later. I trust Jesus as my Savior and choose to follow Him as Lord. Help me live for you. In Jesus' name, I pray. Amen.

What's Next?

If this is the first time you've accepted God's gift of salvation, then welcome to the family! You now know God and He knows you. If you're already a Christ-follower, have a conversation this week that leads a friend closer to the real prize.

Based on Book 2, Day 31

"Why do you call me, 'Lord, Lord,' but do not do what I say?"
Luke 6:46

Day 37

The House that Stands

Builders know the most important part of their job is to get the foundation—the base—of the house right because the whole structure sits on top of it. If the foundation isn't strong, the building will fall.

One day, Jesus shared a parable about a wise builder and a foolish builder.

The wise builder chose rock for his foundation because he knew that storms would eventually come. He wanted to be ready for the wind and the rain, and the destruction they would surely cause.

The foolish builder chose sand for his foundation. Unlike rock that is solid and strong, sand is shaky and shifty. It moves when the wind blows and the rain falls (Matthew 7:24-27).

So, whose house do you think weathered the storms?

Yep. The house that was built on the rock.

Jesus compared a wise builder to those who read their Bibles and obey what it says. Those who take their thoughts to God in prayer and wait to hear His. Those whose very identities are based on His love for them and on the hope of eternal life with Him in heaven.

On the other hand, Jesus compared a foolish builder to those who hear the truth but still don't obey. Those who know deep-down what God wants for their lives, but do what they want to do instead.

Which builder are you?

Are you the wise one who stands strong by trusting Jesus and obeying His Word? Or the foolish one who calls Jesus "Lord" but doesn't do what He says?

Ephesians 5:15-17 warns: "Be very careful how you live. Do not live like those who are not wise. Live wisely [and] use every chance you have for doing good, because these are evil times. So do not be foolish with your lives. But learn what the Lord wants you to do."

With Jesus as your strong foundation, you will weather any storm life brings.

Prayer Time

Praise God for Jesus, the Rock of your salvation (Psalm 62:6-7). Thank Him for His Word and ask Him for strength to put it into practice on a daily basis, so that you can be strong when trials and temptations come.

What's Next?

Think about a time you disobeyed God's clear instruction. What happened when you did not listen to the Lord and obey Him?

Based on Book 2, Day 32

Day 38

All Your Heart

> Jesus answered, "Love the Lord your God with all your heart,
> soul and mind."
> Matthew 22:37

The religious leaders in Jesus' day were always trying to trick Him. But no one can outsmart God. So, when a group of Pharisees asked Jesus which of the commandments was the greatest, He answered, "Love the Lord your God with all your heart, soul and mind. This is the first and most important command" (Matthew 22:37-38).

Jesus knew loving like that was impossible for them.

It's impossible for us too.

Loving God with everything in you can't be done in your sinful nature; it takes a supernatural one. When you put your faith in Jesus

Christ, you get His Holy Spirit—the one who lives in your heart and enables you to love the way you're supposed to.

That's how it works. In fact, the Bible says, "We love because God first loved us" (1 John 4:19).

Sadly, the Pharisees allowed their rules and religious traditions to take up all the space in their hearts. They thought loving God meant being on their best behavior. But they missed the bigger picture because they refused to accept their inability to keep the greatest commandment.

When talking to these church leaders, perhaps Jesus had Isaiah 29:13 on His mind: "These people come near to me with their mouth and honor me with their lips, but their hearts are far from me. Their worship of me is based on human rules they have been taught" (niv).

Jesus wants you to know that nothing and no one should come between you and Him—not even your obedience to Him! In other words, following rules doesn't replace your relationship with Jesus. God is pleased when all the parts of you—your thoughts and actions, your activities and priorities, your feelings and faith—revolve around and flow from your love for Him.

Remember, we love God because God first loved us.

Truth is, knowing how much you're loved should change you from the inside out. Jesus gave His whole self for you on the cross so that you could give your whole self back to Him. And by the power of the Holy Spirit, loving God with your heart, soul, and mind is actually possible.

Prayer Time

Praise the Lord for loving you first and enabling you to love Him back. Confess anything that might be taking up the space in your heart that belongs to Him. Ask for God's love to overflow from you to others, that they might see your deep love for Jesus and want to know Him too.

What's Next?

Our choices matter, but they should be the result of our love for Jesus, NOT the starting place. Look up 1 John 4:9–10 and spend some time really thinking about His love for you.

Based on Book 2, Day 37

Day 39
Compassion

Jesus traveled through all the towns and villages. He taught in their synagogues and told people the Good News about the kingdom. And he healed all kinds of diseases and sicknesses. He saw the crowds of people and felt sorry for them because they were worried and helpless.

They were like sheep without a shepherd.

Matthew 9:35-36

Jesus healed the spots of the leper. He made blind eyes see and weak legs walk. He delivered people from demonic possession and brought others back from the dead.

And He cried because His friends were crying.

Lazarus and his sisters were Jesus' good friends. So, when Lazarus got sick, the women sent word to Jesus to come and heal their brother. But by the time Jesus returned, Lazarus was already dead and everyone was grieving.

"When Jesus saw [Lazarus' sister] weeping, and the Jews who had come with her also weeping, he was deeply moved in his spirit and greatly troubled. And he said, 'Where have you laid him?' They said to him, 'Lord, come and see.' Jesus wept" (John 11:33-35 esv).

Jesus knew He was going to raise Lazarus from the dead—which means Jesus wasn't crying because His friend was gone. He was crying because the people He loved were crying.

Here's the point. Jesus is intimately aware that life on this sin-broken planet can be sad and extremely difficult. That's why He came! He sees you and feels compassion for you because you are worried and hurting and helpless. Without Him, you're like a sheep without a shepherd.

And so, He has tremendous compassion for you. In fact, there is never a time Jesus doesn't know where you are and what you need. The Bible says the helpless call out to Him and He answers, He saves them from all their troubles (Psalm 34:6).

Whatever sadness you're facing today, God is near. He wants you to come to Him and share your truest feelings because He's your loving, living, compassionate Shepherd who understands your pain—pain that He has experienced firsthand.

Like the Good Shepherd He is, Jesus will comfort, lead, rescue, and one day "wipe away every tear" (Revelation 21:4).

You can trust Him.

Prayer Time

Praise God for His care, concern, and compassion that cover every detail of your life. Tell Him how you really feel and ask Him to comfort your heart. Thank Him for grieving with you, and for promising to never leave you alone in your sadness (Deuteronomy 31:8).

What's Next?

1 Peter 5:7 says, "Give all your worries to [God], because he cares for you." What worries, hurt, or struggle do you need to take to the Good Shepherd today?

Based on Book 2, Day 39

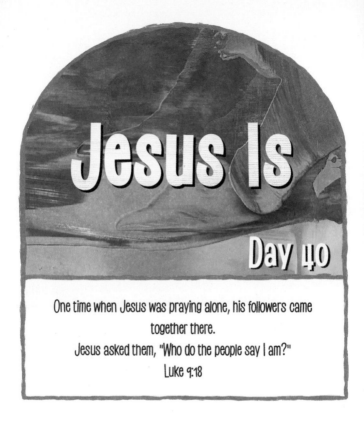

Jesus Is

Day 40

One time when Jesus was praying alone, his followers came together there.
Jesus asked them, "Who do the people say I am?"
Luke 9:18

Sometimes in the Bible, Jesus is called the Good Shepherd. But other times, He's called the Lamb. In fact, one day as Jesus was approaching, John the Baptizer yelled out, "Look, the Lamb of God. He takes away the sins of the world!" (John 1:29)

You see, a lamb was the animal most often used as a sacrifice to remove the sin of God's chosen people. But then Jesus sacrificed *Himself* on the cross so that when we choose to follow Him, our sins are completely wiped away.

Jesus is the Lamb.

Because Jesus rose from the dead three days later, you can be assured that one day you too will rise to life in heaven with the Lord. Jesus said, "I am the resurrection and the life. He who believes in me will have life even if he dies." (John 11:25).

Jesus is the Life.

In fact, God's plan from the beginning of creation was to know you and for you to know Him. *That's* why He's your Good Shepherd. *That's* why He became the Lamb. *That's* why He offers you eternal life—and love—in Him.

"Yes I am sure that nothing can separate us from the love God has for us. Not death, not life, not angels, not ruling spirits, nothing now, nothing in the future, no powers, nothing above us, nothing below us, or anything else in the whole world will ever be able to separate us from the love of God that is in Christ Jesus our Lord" (Romans 8:38-39).

Jesus is Love.

Most importantly, the Bible says, "No one has seen God, but Jesus is exactly like him... And through Christ, God decided to bring all things back to himself again—things on earth and things in heaven. God made peace by using the blood of Christ's death on the cross" (Colossians 1:15, 20).

We didn't get the privilege of walking alongside Jesus like Simon

Peter, Nicodemus, Matthew, and Mary did. But like them, we can know Jesus. And when we know Jesus, we know God—the high King and ruler of heaven and earth.

"Then [Jesus] said to them, 'But who do you say that I am?' And Peter answered, 'The Christ of God'" (Luke 9:20 esv).

Jesus. Is. Lord.

Prayer Time

Praise God for sending Jesus to be your Lamb. And Shepherd. And Life. And Lord. Be honest with Him about any doubts you may still have. Ask Jesus to strengthen your faith and hope in Him.

What's Next?

Answer Jesus' question for yourself: *Who do you say I am?*

Based on Book 2, Day 40